ALL ROADS LEAD TO HERE

VAN K. BROCK
FLORIDA POETRY SERIES
ANHINGA PRESS

ALL ROADS LEAD TO HERE

POEMS

CAROLINA HOSPITAL

VAN K. BROCK
FLORIDA POETRY SERIES
ANHINGA PRESS

TALLAHASSEE, FLORIDA 2026

Copyright © 2026 CAROLINA HOSPITAL All rights reserved under International and Pan-American Copyright Conventions.

No portion of this book may be reproduced in any form without the written permission of the publisher, except by a reviewer, who may quote brief passages in connection with a review for a magazine or newspaper.

Cover art: *Atlantic Seam, Florida 2024*, Photograph by Carolina Hospital
Author photo by Carlos Medina
Design and production: Carol Lynne Knight

Type Styles: Poem texts are set in Adobe Jenson, designed for Adobe Systems by Robert Slimbach. Its Roman styles are based on a text face cut by Nicolas Jenson in Venice around 1470, and its italics are based on those created by Ludovico Vicentino degli Arrighi fifty years later. Jenson is an organic design, with a low x-height. Titles are set in Yana designed by Laura Worthington. She published her first typeface in 2010 and now has more than 200 type designs. The swash is from Charcuterie Ornnaments, also designed by Laura Worthington. The Charcuterie font family is reminiscent of early 1900s graphic styling.

Library of Congress Cataloging-in-Publication Data
"All Roads Lead to Here" by Carolina Hospital, First Edition
ISBN — 978-1-934695-97-5
Library of Congress Control Number: 2026931441

Anhinga Press Inc. is dedicated wholly to the publication and appreciation of fine poetry and other literary genres.

For personal orders, catalogs, and information write to:
Anhinga Press
P.O. Box 3665
Tallahassee, Florida 32315
Website: www.anhingapress.org
Email: info@anhinga.org

Published in the United States
by Anhinga Press
Tallahassee, Florida, 2026

for Carlos

ANHINGA PRESS ADVISORY BOARD

Our thanks to these wonderful poets
for supporting the mission of Anhinga Press —
to publish fine poetry.

Ellen Bass
Richard Blanco
Rick Campbell
Terri Carrion
Denise Duhamel
Dorianne Laux
Naomi Shihab Nye
Virgil Suarez
Terese Svoboda

Carol Lynne Knight, Co-director
Kristine Snodgrass, Co-director
Karla Van Vliet, Co-director
Amber Lunderman, Assistant Editor

ANHINGA PRESS BOARD OF DIRECTORS

Sue Scavo, President
Michael Trammell, Secretary
Craig Beaven, Director
Rafael Gamero, Director
Jennifer Schomburg Kanke, Director
Carlos Miranda, Director
Elizabeth A.I. Powell, Director

CONTENTS

Acknowledgments: xi

      PROLOGUE
Caracoles   3

      I
A New Birth Date   7
Transit Home   8
Runaway Time: Stiltsville over Biscayne Bay   9
Last Picture at Jekyll Island   10
Until Now   11
How I See Things after the Rainstorm   12
Bird (and Frog) Watching   13
Mourning for School Girls in Cerulean Headscarves   14
Acts   15
Be Intoxicated Always in Her Love   16
The Letter F   18
Students Write During the Pandemic: Cento   19
First Responders: Morning after January 6, 2021   20
The Strange Guest   22
Meditations   23
Abandoned Architecture   24
Words → Palabras → Parables   26
The Cello   28
Sunday Outing to Tomoka State Park   29
Trees We Have Planted in Our New Home   31
Magnified Miracles   32
Sanibel   33

II

Crossroads and Borders   37
After a Short-Lived Childhood   38
All Roads Lead to 7   39
Homegrown Claves   40
Mi Historia: A Triptych in Cento   41
Without Fanfare   43
La Virgencita   44
Collares of Blue and White Beads   45
Parting Portraits   46
Soneto for Mozart   47
Banging Pots and Pans   48
Nose-dive into Exile   49
Girlhood: Exorcism   50
Girlhood: The Front Yard   51
The Summer of Johnny, 1975   52
On Mothers: Paintings by Virginie Demont-Breton   53
A Mother's Derecho   54
Waning Landscape   55
If Mother Were a Ship   56
Tending Sisters   57

III

Self-Portrait   61
Creation   63
Two Poems: For When You Love Someone the Way I Love You   64
Waterway   66
Miami Melodies in Late July   67
Love in the Time of Covid   68
Boxed Lace   70
Twined   71

The Wedding Arch   72
Moving Day   73
Of Dreams I Sleep   74
Protecting the Interior   75
Shirts with Bags (Austria, 15th Century)   76
The Cross That Carries Us   78
Rincón de la Vieja National Park: Summer after Cancer   79
Primer for Diagramming Breast Cancer   80
Refracted   81
There Is No Turning   82
Bloodroute   83
Driving Back   85
Under a Still Sky   86
Today I Have Company   87
Going on Five Decades   88
Taking Turns   89

    EPILOGUE
Band of Poets   93

About the Author   94

THANKS & ACKNOWLEDGMENTS:

Thank you, family, from mom and dad, who passed away years ago, to little June and Evie, just starting out. Thank you, Nicole and Sonora, daughters and best friends, who keep me motivated and listen to me, a lot. And to Carlos (Baba), you are the driving force in my life and work.

A special note of thanks to Holly Iglesias, Nicole Hospital-Medina, and especially Maureen Seaton, without whom this book would not exist. Most of the poems in this collection were written during our *Tres abuelas y una mamá* seven-year weekly poetry workshops.

My gratitude to my sisters and friends for your constant encouragement and especially to Mia Leonin, Holly Iglesias, and Geoffrey Philp for your kind and generous words.

Thank you to Nicole Tallman, wise editor and friend, for your support of my work.

And finally, a big thank you to Carol Lynne Knight, with whom it is always a pleasure to collaborate, Kristine Snodgrass, and everyone at Anhinga Press, my literary home.

****

My gratitude and acknowledgement to the editors/directors/staff of these publications, where some of the poems have previously appeared, at times in earlier versions.

The Acentos Review: "Girlhood: Exorcism"
Anacapa Review: "Under a Still Sky"
contemporary haibun online: "Waning Landscape"

Limp Wrist: "Words → Palabras → Parables" and "Last Picture at Jekyll Island"

MER: "On Mothers: Paintings by Virginie Demont-Breton"

[PANK]: "All Roads lead to 7"

South Florida Poetry Journal: "Mourning for Girls with Cerulean Headscarves"

Waxwing: "Caracoles"

Chameleon Chimera / SoFloPoJo: "Magnified Miracles"

Witchery / SoFloPoJo: "Abandoned Architecture"

Rumors, Secrets & Lies: Narrative Poems about Pregnancy, Abortion, & Choice, "Until Now," (Edited by Carol Lynne Knight & Kristine Snodgrass, Anhinga Press, 2022)

Thanks to Anhinga Press where "Refracted," and "Primer for Diagramming Breast Cancer" are included in the collection *How to Get into Trouble*, a collaborative chapbook with Maureen Seaton, Holly Iglesias, and Nicole Hospital-Medina.

PROLOGUE

CARACOLES

for Maureen Seaton

0. In 1614, a caracole described the twists and turns of a horse, its Latin origin spirals, like a snail, a conch, a seashell.

1. A bi-valve clam style shell holds its pressure by its hinge and outer edges, while a spiral screw shaped one does it in its core and wide top.

1. I am a spiral.

2. We used to have a spiral staircase inside our home.

3. Hacer caracoles means to weave about and subir en caracoles to spiral up.

5. How do we stop spiraling out of control?

8. Caracoles! Good Heavens!

13. Growing cabbage isn't hard, so they say. Garden rows of swirls.

21. We officially begin the life-passage into adulthood; the spiral unfolds.

34. The product of 2 prime numbers, 2 X 17, and the age of the oldest of our 2 daughters.

55. Twins in embryo, the forming septum undergoes a gradual spiraling course that ultimately completes into separate aorta and pulmonary arteries.

89. Messier 89 is an elliptical galaxy in the constellation Virgo. I was born in Virgo.

144. *Two loves I have of comfort and despair.*

233. On this magnificent number, I fold.

I

A NEW BIRTH DATE

I always struggled to settle mom's version of events about departing Havana, a tale sculpted from brittle sandstone. Then, my sister frames for me the unearthed plane ticket, a faded handwritten roadmap to the inaccessible memories of a four-year-old, before the plunge. To plunge us into rocks is what mother threatens if the British officer refuses us the permit into Jamaica. Without it, I (a Miamian) would have been yo (la de La Habana), like my cousin Lisset. Across the bottom of the promised voucher, someone has printed my name. Issued by K.L.M. Royal Dutch Airlines from Havana to Kingston and back to Havana, the ticket poses the narrative of a Caribbean getaway. The date of approval is stamped July 4, 1961. At the Malecón, mother offers ofrendas for the Dutch miracle, the last flight out of Havana. Flight # 978 departs from Rancho-Boyeros Airport two weeks later, with mother clutching three daughters. Father has left earlier on a prearranged work scheme. She doesn't breathe until we land in Kingston, until we see our father, until we all finally make our way to San Juan. A 5-year pit stop before Miami, the finish line. Mom and dad never look back. That burden is mine.

TRANSIT HOME

after the painting "Spiral Transit" by Remedios Varo

The medieval village interconnects through towers and walls.
It coils, like a nautilus, with helm roofs or sloped turrets marking
each curve. It dominates choppy waves under low storm clouds.

The burnt orange spiral spins   spins   spins   spins   spins

off the canvas.   I swallow it.

I am Remedios Varo. We are the labyrinth where the hollow seed
sailboats navigate towards the bird belfry, in the serpentine gyre.
We come from Girona, a family of engineers, draftsmen, and artists.

We consume   Hieronymus Bosch   El Greco   Marc Chagall.

Our name is exile.   We walk the maze.

It transforms into a hard-empty shell I must vomit back out.
It lands in the current, the boats, the waves, the clouds, my head
whirling. Drawn in behind the gondolas, I cannot turn away.

RUNAWAY TIME: STILTSVILLE OVER BISCAYNE BAY

Flames engulf the wooden beams
that snap and tumble
on concrete pilings
      10 feet above
           the shallow flats
clear turquoise bay

I visited the house twice
once by day
      a cool crystal dive
another by night
      a moonlit gallery

Six remain from 25
in 1933 "Crawfish" Eddie Walker
built the first
      bait and chum,
      and a bit of booze for luck

LAST PICTURE AT JEKYLL ISLAND

Once the verdant forest reached
the shore. Now stripped trees rise
among fallen trunks and upturned
roots, like exposed hearts, larger

than me and you. Gray weathered
stumps with barks of elephant seal
skins design sculptures on the sand,
slanted branches flowing like wind,

a tangled Dios pointing to the sky,
a fitting place to end our road trip
circling Georgia, on the morning
the highest court strips our rights

meandering over battered remains
on a stunning driftwood cemetery.

UNTIL NOW

As the judges argue the case, I accompany my unwed teenage friend, to an apartment building in Little Havana. In the black Monte Carlo, I wait, my thoughts ricocheting between her safety, my complicity, and the fate of both our souls. I am terrified, having spent 12 years in parochial school, listening to warnings from the sisters, and my mother.

Decades later, after I become a mother and mami, a grandmother, she erupts a confession: my Catholic mother had an abortion. In exile in 1961, with nothing but three daughters, ages five months to seven years old, she trudges alone, down a dark alley into a filthy room. She suffocates this truth, until she can't. At first, I am furious with her generational secret, then grace and memories intervene. Before I got married at 18, she made sure I was equipped with proper birth control, so I am grateful. Never did I have to confront her gut-wrenching choice, nor that of my friend's, nor society's stigma, nor the terror of the law.

HOW I SEE THINGS AFTER THE RAINSTORM

Men (not all men) design atom bombs they regret
and forge alliances between bishops and fascists and

accumulate gold to fill a drain field or maybe two.
They make themselves feel grand because they are

learned or cunning or own a semi (weapon or truck)
or a woman-on-the back Harley. They surge over

neighborhoods, the force of a tsunami or tornado.
Women (not all women) rail against false convictions

or neglect of children, sometimes hunted down like prey.
Their rage spills down hills into rivers and lakes, farms and

fields. It turns into a weeping bottlebrush for hummingbirds
or an oak by a porch that calls blue jays and cardinals home.

BIRD (AND FROG) WATCHING

By the boardwalk, the cormorant above the mangrove
fans its wings towards me and the sun, inhaling universe.

The ibis seems content foraging in shallow light
its downcurved bill sweeping the brackish marsh.

After stalking and stabbing the killifish with its sharp beak,
the white necked anhinga, safely perched, scans below.

At home, I lift one of the stacked Adirondack chairs. A lone frog,
a Southern Chorus, is sucked to the chairback. It's gone when I

return, so I lift another. The frog has squeezed itself between slats
until it finally springs towards the grass. Could this be the one

that swam across the backyard lake formed by the storm surge?
It's all so much easier for the plumed ones.

MOURNING FOR SCHOOL GIRLS IN CERULEAN HEADSCARVES

I cannot write about the pelicans on shore flying in V-formation,
nor the buried sunflowers and sea oats on the protected sand dunes,
not today. They disguise fighter jets, land mines, and trenches.

A car bomb and two other blasts detonate near the school gates,
the first so powerful, and so close, some children cannot be found.

I cannot write about daughters and granddaughters, safely sheltered,
ringed by myths, fables, and princess coloring books, like the one
strewn on the dusty street next to torn notebooks and bloodied sneakers.

The afternoon shift of high school girls is the target, 85 dead,
another 147 maimed or wounded by shrapnel tearing their bodies.

I cannot write about college girls in my classes who outnumber the boys
nor about the emails from former students in graduate school. Not today.
Today I can only sob for this loss so distant, of youth, of hope, of God.

On the arid hilltop near Kabul, hundreds gather to mourn their daughters.
By the dirt graves, they defiantly scribe large white letters: EDUCATION.

ACTS

CONTRITION:

Blame the words. They jump hurdles to spit out half truths before the world spins and splinters apart.

Blame the words. They spray paint over rust and cracks, hide air bubbles, until steel fails and concrete overflows.

Blame me and only me. I conjure up masks of syllables to trick the wounds and melt the scabs before dessert.

Blame me and only me. I turn a phrase to desire, a verb to an oath. Mercy deconstructs a lifetime of tablecloths.

LOVE:

Blame me and only me.

BE INTOXICATED ALWAYS IN HER LOVE
(Proverbs 5:19)

The young priest at our dining table
inhaling picadillo and Merlot, like a fetish,
exclaims *Catholics are obsessed with sex.*

What do you mean?
I refill the brandy snifter.

premarital sex
gay sex
adultery sex
immoral sex
teen sex
virginal sex

Thoughts swell my brain
a laser beam fired through crystal
a quantum entanglement
an eon flash
la petite morte, iku
resurrection
Už budu, I will be
omnipotent
Ēl

What's the answer?
El Señor, he says, before leaving.

When I was 9, the Lord's Prayer breathed
Padre Nuestro que estás en el cielo …
It still feels like going home en español.

El Señor, mister with a capital M, is mute.
If I am called to accept el patriarcado,
I choose, not a Mister, erect and aloof,
but a devoted Father, better yet, a unisex
God with all-out love, a knack for delight,
and a sense of humor.

Oh God, my partner exhales,
in my ear.

THE LETTER F

The letter F feels so final, but on the page looks half a letter,
incomplete, an unfinished door frame. The letter F has been
usurped by Failure. Even Fuck, which probably emerged from
the Swedish copulate
or penis or the Middle
English fiddle or flirt
or the German itch or scratch, sounds like faulty sex, as if in
making love, the letter L was erased. The letter F forgets and
creates fissure. I never do give my students Fs on their essays.
D will do. It
carries hope,
like a dog or
a daisy or a
daiquiri or dawn.
That's as long as
I don't let myself
think about
Disaster. But
this is about
the F. I will
try to befriend
it, will search
memories of
Sunday funnies,
gold freesias,
sea foam and
first kisses.

STUDENTS WRITE DURING THE PANDEMIC: CENTO

for all my students

The curandera has wisdom sewn within her wrinkles.
I sit at her table as she crushes bitter truths in her mortar.
Sometimes a morning is just a morning.
Find me somewhere among the clouds.
When he asks me to ride the hang gliders, I say yes,
when I'd rather say no. I dare try it.
In anything but name, I feel like a dropout,
parts I have played in the plot.
Looking at the parts we hide
I don't know you well enough to whisper your name.
Hating myself has grown tiring,
something inside anchored in the roaring waves.
I am a thesis, a failed art piece.
Please don't bury me in the garden.

From my creative writing class at Miami Dade College, Spring 2020: lines 1-2 Isaac Pizarro, lines 3-4 Isabella Ramirez, lines 5-6 Stephanie Trujillo, lines 7-8 Arturo Girona, lines 9-10 Alexa Velez, lines 11-12 Andrew Rothman, and lines 13-14 Sofia Valdeón.

FIRST RESPONDERS: MORNING AFTER JANUARY 6, 2021

The new students arrive, strangers.
At first, they respond with images

Mobs scaling walls	Dangling ropes	
A Wave of Red hats		Zip ties
	Confederate flags waving	
Banners	Pounding on smashed glass	
	Profane Threats	
Shaman in horns		
Noose	Crushed policeman	

then the words trickle out

Horror	Digest Disgrace	
Heartbreak		
	Anger	Helplessness
Fear	Sadness	
Distress		Shock
Anxiety	Violation	
Shame		Rage

until an exhausted
silence betrays them.

Black letters
wailing against
the whiteboard

dress wounds
shield tears
restore breath.

We are not strangers.

THE STRANGE GUEST

The red shouldered hawk swoops down over the back deck
straight toward me behind the glass. I stand, fixed on its wide
banded wings. Before impact, it turns, flies to its usual perch
on a dead oak branch. It takes a minute to realize, I lost a dare.

*

Beneath the jeep, the gopher tortoise rests.
When it senses my footsteps, it ambles toward the swale,
stops to eat some berries. Then it darts to find its hidden
burrow, a surprising flash of speed in slow and steady time.

*

Above the high grass, the black racer lifts its head.
We make eye contact, I think. It flees beneath the sunflowers
by the porch. I back away quickly. Fear is a strong ignorance.

*

I watch its long stick-like legs guardedly entering our side lawn.
The Great White Egret's curved neck sways, scrutinizes, dagger bill
at the ready. I freeze. It steps onto the porch, past the hammock.
Slowly, it walks away from my dream house, unimpressed.

MEDITATIONS

I first saw Queen Ann's lace grow wildly along the highway
on our way to the mountains, where I also saw phosphorescent

dragonflies and lavender rhododendron. At our new home,
I never tire of the yellow beach sunflowers along the dunes.

I usually see random weeds during my walks, with tiny
blossoms you hardly notice. Then one springs up with color

or an unusual alien orchid shape. The flora here can startle.
The tides grant jolts. I track daily charts, like Eliot measures

coffee spoons. At the peak, the waves break so high, it's hard
to walk, but the water spreads over the rocks like waterfalls.

Low tides also come gifted, exposing sea glass shards,
ancient shark teeth, or coquina sculptures. Foam floats

over the shoreline like baby's breath. Each day is a lifetime.

ABANDONED ARCHITECTURE
after Abraham Lincoln Lewis & MaVynee Betsch "The Beach Lady"

Driving along A1A, we collect landscapes like sea glass on the shore
the car on the ferry
the St. John's River
Little Talbot marshes
Amelia Island live oaks.
At Fort Clinch
he combs the sand
for shark teeth,
I visit memories across water
butterflies and wild horses
at Cumberland Island.
On our way back
we search for American Beach
along streets lined with mansions
until many begin to show signs
of disrepair. Then NaNa's Dune,
the tallest in Florida,
in a field of dune daisies. Sixty feet rising across what used to thrive
a black beach community
summer hotels, sandwich shops,
Evan's Ocean Rendezvous.
Some memories are not mine
to reconstruct, but I can't help
imagining these empty streets,
once filled with cars and buses,
sand packed with umbrellas,
Model A Fords and Panama hats,
Duke Ellington and Cab Callaway.
After hurricanes and desegregation,
what remains are falling ceilings,

peeling walls, old pianos, rusty jars,
a moldy Jutte box and a long
promise of reconstruction.
MaVynee's ashes at the top,
the sand dune she rescued remains, a beacon with a dimming light.

WORDS → PALABRAS → PARABLES

the male is an incomplete female
— Valerie Solanas

1.

His → tory
His → torian
Hys → teria
Hys → terectomy
Hysterical Hysterectomy
Man → ly
Man → ifest
Man → ifesto
Man → made
Man → acle
Sola → nas
Sola
Her → story

2.

Matanzas → Massacre
Massacre River
Massacre Bay
Massacre Beach
Massacre Inlet
Massacre State Forrest
Fort Massacre
Massacre Wildlife Management
Massacre High School
Massacre on the Bay Bar and Grill

3.

Femelle ≠ Masle
Hominen → human
Humus → earth/dust/mud
Hum → ility
Fer → tility
Wo → man
Woe → man
Wow → man
Fe → male
Fe → iron
Fe → trust
Feliz

THE CELLO
after Pablo Casals and Federico García Lorca

before a long sleep
Song of the Birds
taking flight
        over the olive trees
        over La Sagrada Familia
before crossing the Pyrenees
in the depth of night
gliding strings
        over vineyards
        over sand and asphalt
a steady
slow
drizzle
the bow trembles
        over flat waters
        over empty canvases
again and again
pleading
        peace
        peace
        peace

SUNDAY OUTING TO TOMOKA STATE PARK
after Kimiko Hahn

On the way, we pass Bulow Creek. Streams and bogs, cabbage palms and mossy oaks. You are wearing the fundraising t-shirt for the endangered creek. Mega-Development.

You must not lose faith in humanity. Humanity is like an ocean; if a few drops of the ocean are dirty, the ocean does not become dirty. (Gandhi)

More than 1,500 of the 5,600 acres of Bulow Park are submerged lands.

Roving creek by grassy
coastal marsh. Quiet veil for
slavery and war.

Tomoka State Park's Outpost is a small throwback store, with chairs overlooking the river. It rents canoes and kayaks, as well as sells camping supplies and souvenirs.

Aged white jeep alone
in the parking lot, no more
mail to deliver.

We hike through pines as wide as those on Lake Santa Fe, where we lived through college in two relocated wooden houses, one a store, the other officers' quarters from Camp Blanding. The pines rise in between old, crooked oaks and hickory trees. I breathe slowly. The Timucua chose this site for their village Nocoroco, next to the Halifax River, protected by a barrier island, to easily catch shellfish and hunt deer. Cooler air sneaks through the thicket as we reach the peninsula's point.

Shorelines at the interface of marine, estuarine, and terrestrial biomes are among the most threatened habitats.

Seawalls don't work!

Oyster shells in nets
form a breakwater reef
habitat for crabs.
Mangrove seedlings grow stilts
high where land and water meet.

The fisherman with his young family settles at the point. The mother smiles at my greeting in Spanish. He hooks a pink stingray pup. Carefully he carries it back to the point and releases it.

You hit the brakes in the middle of the road home. A white tail deer eyes us from the swale. Her fawn runs back through the foliage. Future site for a new community. Golf, anyone?

Dawn crests the tree line.
Bamboo windchimes. Crashing waves.
I unravel mat
and stretch into memory
of Tomoka's river breeze.

TREES WE HAVE PLANTED IN OUR NEW HOME

Seven live oaks

>Birds often build nests on our young oaks. Today two mocking birds carry twigs from the ground inside the thick foliage. They chase other birds away.

One red maple

>Originally, we planted three, but two died. The third has branches so wide, green is all we can see from the kitchen window. I wish maples didn't bare themselves in winter.

One weeping bottlebrush

>Hummingbirds, butterflies, bees and I love its flower spikes. The scarlet stamens hang from the tips of the weeping branches, stirring encounters.

Three Simpson's stoppers

>We had never heard of these small threatened native trees, with their orange berries and tiny white flowers, until we planted them in the backyard. They have finally reached the top of the wooden fence.

Eight seagrapes

>They form a bright green screen, necklace chains of large round leaves with red veins adorning the garden.

Twenty Graceful bamboos

>Bamboos are really grasses, but their canes grow tall like trees. In the breeze, their flowing leaves awaken the sea.

One magnolia

>After our road trip to Georgia, we fall in love with its sturdy leaves and wide white blossoms.

One olive

>Far from its origins, it is thriving in our backyard. It has grown accustomed to the landscape, like us.

MAGNIFIED MIRACLES

I know of nothing else but miracles.
           — Walt Whitman

I do not understand their making, but there they are

when I walk beneath a dome of royal
    poinciana blooms to peek at the sky

    bike ride through a dense mangrove
        forest that bursts into bay

    wade in the shallows at low tide, as sea
        foam cushions my bare feet

    follow a squirrel scurrying from post
        to post across a high wire

    spot a ruby-throated hummingbird that
        shimmers against the firebush

    await the full moon to carve a wake
        of light over the dark swells

    feel the weightlessness of a child
        asleep on my shoulder

    sway to Santana with the one I love

Every breath is a miracle
Every atom   Watch them kiss

SANIBEL

wind kissed and quiet
from our honeymoon start
        you threw a lifeline to our future
            and now our past
a shallow bank of shells
        you gifted us
            tender armor
a wildlife hideaway for pinks
        new colors to hold
            flamingoes and spoonbills
for years we inhaled your sea breaths
        without the high rises
            or the fast foods
yet so swiftly you are breached and blown
        and we drown in the swells
            uprooted again
vulnerable but magnificent
        in need of resurrection
            island mirror in the sun
wind kissed and quiet

CROSSROADS AND BORDERS

Who wouldn't want to bottle their color,
so alluringly beyond blue you want to name it hope...
    from "Potatoes" by Barbara Ras

The ocean is a giant bottle of color.

I was born on an island surrounded
by spectacular shades of hope, uprooted
by those who can't distinguish indigo from black.

Fire emerges red above orange
above yellow. Yellow unfolds into sun
and sun sets into moon.

We depart the city for a house by the sea
beneath a wet moon.

A mother with her six-year-old child asks
the reporter on the streets of Kyiv: where
should we go? where is safe? the apartment?
the subway tunnel? the countryside? Poland?
Her voice exhales sunflowers.

Sixty years ago, our mother yanked us
out of this island flanked by blues
and flew us into purple.

How many bottles must spill until we are empty
of colors?

AFTER A SHORT-LIVED CHILDHOOD

Lately, I've been thinking about the days when I felt most isleña.
They slide off my palms into the waves. You say everything
we have done since we first married lead to this house by the sea.
Our Sanibel honeymoon many years ago and all the return trips,

the copper bamboo fountain hauled from the Keys, the four post
bed with mosquitero, our visits to Elbow Cay, D.R. and Costa Rica,
the shell collections, the Buddhist bell, the college house on mossy
oaks Lake Santa Fe at the same latitude. Here, we make the mojitos

under the maple tree listening to Willy and Celia. Is this homeland?
not the mythical (to me) Caribbean island of my birth? Grandfather
was Catalan & I danced flamenco and played castanets growing up,
so is that peninsula patria? From one lifetime to another, where do

we leave behind God's Country? Is the quest the journey or purpose?
Do we forage the past or its future? Or does the chase end at the sea?

ALL ROADS LEAD TO 7

Surf Drive, 7 around the pandemic table, sobremesa every
night, with the girls growing up, with partners and babies now.

Born on day 27 of year 7, after God made the universe by day
7 to rest in sacredness and spiritual perfection. Could I be perfect?

En la charada cubana, the 7 is a shell or Yemaya, la Virgen de Regla.
I used to play the piano scales, in Western music based on 7 notes.

Light passed through a prism split into 7 parts. In the Bible, 7 appears
more than 700 times without counting sevenfold, 70 or 700.

In Confucianism 7 is a combination of yin and yang and 5 elements:
metal, wood, water, fire, and earth, together in harmony in Taoism.

Every 7 years changes occur in the body. We have 7 bones in the face,
neck, and ankle, and 7 holes in our head. There are 7 crystal systems.

My fifth, throat, chakra, one of the 7, is definitely unbalanced, or maybe
it's my third eye. I will write these words in turquoise and sing them later.

The 7 colors of the rainbow, the 7 days of the week, a prime number.
Seven used to be siete, which sounds like cielo; I was siete in San Juan.

At siete, I didn't understand how far I would travel from my prime;
we have composed a new melody, under watch of the Seven Sisters.

HOMEGROWN CLAVES

Cuttings from the bamboo planted
last summer spread along the fence.
Eucalyptus green culms calling with

short, short, long, short, long
short, short, long, short, long

smoothness. My palms sweep cool stems.
Next to my journal, they easily dry into two
hollow sticks, tapping one another. A sharp

short, short, long, short, long
short, short, long, short, long

clicking, ancient yet familiar. I shift my hold,
alter strike locations, hollowness amplifying
over and over, until the beats grow into son.

short, short, long, short, long
short, short, long, short, long

Tension | release from enslaved Africans in Cuba
to Florida, ship pegs make blood driving música.

MI HISTORIA: A TRIPTYCH IN CENTO

I

The sea has paralyzed its waves
and rapid seagulls split the air.
I have two patrias, Cuba and the night.
The night is good to say goodbye,

to wrench me from my earth,
hoists sails, and ready winds.
Compose your pain though it's already too late.
Water… Water …Water… Coming in through the cracks.
The shoreline drowns in the vapors.
I know he is alive.
One day islands will flow downstream;
bones will dance over the waves.

II

My pleasant things in ashes lie.
The world no longer let me love
and now we roam in Sovereign Woods –
for I have but the power to kill.
The spotted hawk swoops by and accuses me;
I resist anything better than my own diversity.
Saxophone cry that shivered the cities down to the last radio,
a nightmare, bodies turned to stone as heavy as the moon,
we tied branches to our helmets.
We hugged bamboo and leaned.
There is no loneliness like theirs.
I would like to hold the slenderer one in my arms.
If I say *el azul,* you may not see the color
of *mi cielo, mi mar.* Look once upon my sky.

III

In the sky there is nobody asleep. Nobody, nobody.
Life is not a dream. Careful! Careful! Careful!
I don't want to give any sign of what I'm living though
as it comes and goes with my blood.
The soul unfolds itself, like a lotus of countless petals
and forget not that the earth delights to feel.
When the sky is not downcast
and the fields aren't swaying in fright
bring a strongly woven basket.
Flowers now adorn the ground.
The moon rushes through rifted clouds.
I look back. I see
heavy chains and anchors kicking in.
In fact, everything regains its equilibrium.

Every two lines are taken from the following poets I admire from I. Cuba: Julian del Casal, José Martí, Gertrudis Gomez de Avellaneda, Reinaldo Arenas, Heberto Padilla, Roberto Valero. II. North America: Anne Bradstreet, Emily Dickinson, Walt Whitman, Allen Ginsberg, Yusef Komunayakka, James Wright, and Judith Ortiz Cofer. III. The World: Federico García Lorca, Gabriela Mistral, Kahlil Gibran, Anarudha Bhattacharyya, Micere Mugo, Hitomaro, Sinead Morrissey

WITHOUT FANFARE

The building long demolished, the supper club once hailed a 2-story neon sign, Les Violins, ringed by pastel blue and pink diamond stars and the silhouette of a showgirl with feathered wings. Abuelo, member of the house band, had died by the time I was old enough to catch the Las Vegas style pageant, with a Cuban pitch.

After his exile, our Miami house mellowed with the rich sounds of his violin. I only saw him perform once at a rehearsal of the Philharmonic Orchestra at the Olympia Theater. Often at odds with each other, papi and I snuck up to the balcony under a starlit ceiling. As the concerto floated up, papi's face softened. Six months later, abuelo was afflicted by a pancreatic cancer he never knew was terminal. Time follows us without warning.

Without abuelo and now papi, I hold only snippets, such as when Jascha Heifetz broke a string in his Stradivarius, at the Teatro Auditorium, and abuelo, first violinist, lent him his; or of when Alejo Carpentier wrote about abuelo in *Carteles*, of his travels in Europe and playing for Josephine Baker in the French Riviera. One measure at a time, a movement.

LA VIRGENCITA

At 93, our names can baffle her, but not the details of that afternoon at 13, when a salesman knocks at her home in La Habana Vieja, peddling silver Madonnas. Religious icons were not customary in her house, yet the 18-inch Virgin of Charity, baby in arms, skirted by angels and sailors, drives her longing. Her older brother, who later dies in a tragic jeep accident on the family farm in Las Villas, stops by to find her sad. He tracks down and buys the sterling figure. The adolescent turned woman carries her brother's gift to her married suburban house. Years later she hides the statue in my sister's toy bag, as we flee.

From country to country, the virgin hovers over mom's dresser. It is always graced by a burning candle, flowers, a plate piled high with torn photographs, promesas she vows to keep, her chain with a cross and for added protection an azabache. The objects of this world offer her slight assurance for the next. The virgin's star halo, snapped off, totters on her veiled head, like mother's tested devotion. Now bedridden and frail, living in a daughter's bedroom, few artifacts of her life remain. Mother watches her television, right next to this immaculate 80-year-old metal miracle.

COLLARES OF BLUE AND WHITE BEADS

She hid them from us under her blouse. I assumed Brigida had given her the necklaces. Brigida, the daughter of enslaved Cubans, helped raise mother in Manaca, a town in the interior of the island. Already old, living in a backyard casita, Brigida gave her a first taste of divinity and divination. Mother loved Brigida, invoking her name like an incantation.

My search for the beads leads me to my older sister's revelation. She and mother (behind my father's back) take a taxi to Regla. There Cuza grazes her forehead with an ocean stone, while anointing her to Yemayá, the black Virgen de Regla. She entrusts her with a blue and white eleke, like my mother's. Listening to my sister, the enigmas scattered around the houses of my youth flare up: the plate of honey before the virgencita, the untouchable glass of water above the fridge, the protective azabaches, the dry coconuts, the camphor blocks.

Mother begins to unravel. I had dismissed how deep-rooted her beliefs, in spite of her fears. Even today, she hesitates when I press. She laments misplacing her necklaces, along with so many memories, but she recalls the last time she saw Brigida, the night before her wedding. Brigida helped her pack a dowry of new clothes bundled with a secret legacy. When I ask why she never saw Brigida again, mom shrugs her shoulders: *youth, I suppose.*

PARTING PORTRAITS

One print of three wooden skiffs afloat on a crystal calm surf,
in soft pastels, we bought for my father-in-law, the jetsetter,
life of the party, Cuban Mad Men executive, who rum charmed
his way through many lives, including mine, and even the staff

at the nursing home, where he remained after the throat cancer
that left him with a feeding tube, still jovial, watching his boats.
The other, a poster of a bullfighter, my father framed as a gift
after our 1972 visit to Madrid, when I was 14 and rudderless.

When he took us to la corrida, dazzled by the sequined Spaniard
subduing the bull, a red cape tango, I couldn't help looking away.
My father, the introverted engineer, who designed light patterns,
until he didn't, expected me to understand the spectacle, el honor.

The two frames hang side by side in homage to our fathers, both
exiled from patria, an asymmetrical pair, like a gibbous moon.

SONETO FOR MOZART

When you wrote your aria Non più andrai for the first act,
so Figaro could mock the flirtatious Cherubino, compel him
to live like a soldier, to abandon his fine feathers for a helmet,
were you imagining the spoils of war or its stench?

While you sat at your keys before a Vienna audience of palace
vanities, could you envision the gasps of battle across a vast ocean
a century later? Through applause, could you imagine the melody
hummed by many, rifles ready, while Perucho wrote its lyrics?

Cherubino does not march to a military glory. But Perucho's hymn
at Bayamo drives the nation in combat, his prescient verses,
his own fall by a firing squad: he shouts *Morir por la patria es vivir!*
Tell me Mozart, must death be the only choice?

Death's daughter, who hoisted the freedom flag, hides in the woods.
She births nine children and a nation hailing you in anthem march.

BANGING POTS AND PANS

cousin asks us about the Diversity Visas
    at first she hunted down a coyote
        to trek from Nicaragua to Río Grande

scared off by death statistics
    she will take her chances with el bombo
        the least I can do here is fill out the form

immigration lottery
    one month
        millions
            fifty-five thousand
                randomly selected
prize: green cards

Revolución → 63 years
    blackouts and bare bodegas
        doorways of crumbs
            nothing changes nor the will to flee
←Devolución

maybe luck will finally visit my cousin
    I will light a few candles
        and set a glass of water in the corner
            quizás she will be among the chosen

after drowning, you stop fearing the dark
    even the sky feels helpless

NOSE-DIVE INTO EXILE

before summer vacation ends
before our fourth sister is born

the three of us dissolve into the back seat
a red Plymouth Satellite

rounding Florida
road trip

first stop
Silver Springs' glass bottom boats

mom and dad's battles are bottomless

second stop
Weeki Wachee mermaids

their quarrels sink like sirens

third stop
Cypress Gardens towering water skiers

mother flings us into a film reel

last stop
Hollywood motel with kitchenette

nymphets, we plunge into pool water

at last, silence

GIRLHOOD: EXORCISM

Stand in front of a mirror, close your eyes,
and slowly recite five times:

Greñas   (mop of hair)

Desgreñada   (disheveled)

Barriga indecente   (indecent belly)

Barrigona   (big bellied)

Fondillona   (big butted)

Nalgona   (butt-cheeky)

Bocona   (loudmouthed)

Glotona   (glutton)

Gordiflona   (fat)

Raquítica   (scrawny)

Fresca   (rude)

Descuidada   (sloppy)

Descarada   (shameless)

Now, open your eyes, write the words down,
drown them in a jar and freeze them.

(*Ok, mami. Rest in peace.*)

GIRLHOOD: THE FRONT YARD

The back with its swings was predictable.
Me, I always preferred the front yard

where I spread out and rolled over grass
or scraped my knees running until dusk

where I mastered my bike on the street
a bit farther each time reaching the 7-11

where the neighbor requested my services
to babysit her kids for pay (my first "job")

where the sirens from cop cars and firetrucks
alerted me to tragedy and mystery nearby

where boys picked me up for dates, one taking
me to dinner to share he had enlisted, another

to the beach on a day so windy we escaped from
needle like sand to the car (where he groped me)

where my father in striped pj's paced in the dark
until I returned past curfew (we didn't speak)

where I snatched a view of you (who will end up
my spouse) on your way home from work.

THE SUMMER OF JOHNNY, 1975

He was a boy back from our war, not a Cuban Rambo, more like a big blue crab. We had just met in my first college class, a friend of a friend; I felt anxious, but bold. I was driving him home in my parents' red Ford station wagon, windows down, blasting sound, when he asked me to stop at the Mercy Hospital seawall. Until the sun set over the shallow bay, we talked of our families, growing up, school plans. No mention of rice paddy terrain, land mines, or helicopters. I was too artless, too young to sense his distress. He leaned in to kiss me. I could not reciprocate. I awaited another boy, away not in war, but in life making. He didn't press me; for that I was grateful. At his place, friends sat on the floor circling joints.

Much later, I heard that he left town, not knowing he would have been a father had his girl not arrested the pregnancy. I heard that he was living in New York City, in and out of clinics. I heard that he was homeless; even though, his disability checks arrived at his parents' house regularly. Finally, I heard that he had died, alone, without a kiss, or a prayer. The jellyfish-like details of that afternoon with him slide through my fingers, but somehow at an unexpected moment, one stings me and drags me back to the year my ground shifted.

ON MOTHERS: PAINTINGS BY VIRGINIE DEMONT-BRETON

Rough stones piled into walls around her, a bride in white
with veil, *Alma Mater*, sits, her infant on her lap sleeping,
no sign of his fate, but for a halo glowing over his head.
She watches, her lean arms open, a lace tent framing him.

Behind, an alcove, its flaked plaster bright blue. Above, wooden
cross planks carrying the weight of what's missing. At her feet,
yellow and purple wildflowers guarding her exquisite nature.
Best to summon the *Fisherman's Wife*, with firm arms and steady

calves hauling boys out of the sea, balancing over sharp boulders.
She harbors what's hers, like angels who scoop up Mary's house
in Nazareth away from invaders. On their way to Italy, they drop
bits over the lands. In every doorway we hang her metal plaque.

La Virgen de Loreto like the *Mother and Child* (frolicking)
in Waves, she guarantees our safety and that of our homes.

A MOTHER'S DERECHO

after Tada Chimako

Sometimes the body feels like a summer storm
with branch bending squalls and thunderous cracked skies.

My daughter's breasts confirm the damage, the raw cracks,
as she carries on feeding her newborn until she falls asleep.

Our mother never nursed us. Her doctor insisted
formula was the favored option. I wonder if her body

could have endured the weather-beaten turns,
the smarting grasps, the cursory latches, like ours.

Her feeble conceits fail her now, so she grabs at a gust
to steady herself. *I have a magical brain,* she tells us.

I will not die, and I believe she believes that.
In garbled words, she adds. *How will I help them then?*

What will I leave my daughters when I die?
On its way, in this dry calm, a hint of faint wind.

WANING LANDSCAPE

The 400-year-old Fairchild Oak, at the southern end of the trail to the Bulow Plantation Ruins Historic Park, ushers us in. Its 12-foot wide trunk rises up 78 feet, and its long heavy boughs, draped in Spanish moss and resurrection fern, reach over 200 ft across. Circling this spectacular tree, I am struck by sorrow and loss. Perhaps it is the massive broken limbs on the ground. Perhaps it has nothing to do with the tree, but with the fact that Norman Harwood most likely committed suicide under it in the 1880s, decades after the Second Seminole War battered this land. Or perhaps it's that the color of its worn-down branches and its open boughs call up my husband's great-great grandmother's crucifix hanging in our hallway, a resurrected relic. Or maybe it's that our daughter phones to say they set up oxygen tubes for mother after her most recent stroke. We speak about accepting death, then follow the old Seminole route towards the creeks' calming waters.

sweetgum leaves -
falling from furrowed trunks
stars to steer our trek

IF MOTHER WERE A SHIP

She would be a rugged Spanish galleon laid up in peacetime,
timbers weathered and cracked, sails tattered and threadbare.

How her hand trembles now, struggling to dip the Cuban toast
into her café con leche. She refuses our help. She cannot walk

or do much for herself but this early morning task she awaits.
She whispers, I'm not getting better, with an uncommon tone

of finality. I touch her hand and hair, reach to kiss her brow.
Two weeks pass, finally free from vanity and the indignities

of her body, relief slams her, also my younger sister, earnest
caretaker until the end, and all of us, witnessing her slow decay,

like that massive galeón stripped for scraps before it sinks.
Six months later, I still harbor the locked strongbox of her loss.

I begin to sort through a rusted chest of memories from years
before her fall, so I can grieve. She was flawed and formidable.

Willful and sturdy, she defied gales to carry us into exile.
She judged harshly, yet loved us deeply, her emerald eyes

focused on us until her doldrum days. This is the mother I miss.
We are more than the end. She is more than the sum of her end.

TENDING SISTERS

1.

My youngest sister plants a gardenia shrub near the window
where mother spends her last few years bedridden, where she holds
her hands like broken wings, until they part, each to either side
of the unknown river.

2.

Mother takes flight without insistence.

3.

The blue urn will dissolve in the current.

4.

Once Dad handed me a gardenia blossom from their garden.

5.

The 1945 Cuban bolero "Dos Gardenias" becomes a hit
when recorded by La Sonora Matancera.

6.

My sister's new gardenia plant is her offering.

7.

She will blossom without our parents' whirlwind.

8.

Sorting through photos, clippings, and garments,
sister is slowly untangling herself.

9.

I want to dissolve her grief in mine.

III

SELF-PORTRAIT

after Adam Zagajewski and Heberto Padilla

Between warrior poses, tea cups, and watering cans,
my morning passes quickly. But soon I am back
to the computer for essays to grade or verses to edit
until that too ends.
I live between two cities fringed by the sea.
I know this poem will end by the sea
because that is where I will end.
My old neighbors are strangers. My new ones are friends,
or at least friendly when we briefly cross paths.
I read (too much) and paint (for fun) and cook.
My favorite poets teach me to pay attention to the details.
In one city I feel like a palm tree reaching into brightness,
in the other like an oak stretching into shade.
I need movement: biking or dancing, even cleaning or weeding.
I prefer long hikes along the shore or deep in the woods,
where I sense echoes in sea glass and stumps.
Lizards are always scurrying around our bamboos and seagrapes.
Cuba, where I was born, is dominated by lizards,
so many species camouflaged by habitat (& habit),
brown on ground, green on leaf.
This week thousands of unarmed protestors take to the streets
across this lizard shaped island. Bus loads transport rapid-reaction
brigades and party militants armed with bats and sticks.
They manage to lock them in and us out.
I am a child of the ocean and right now I want to see it crash.
I love watching my granddaughters play imagination
with Baba, an essential trait in these trying times.
Their mother, my daughter, was born among Florida lizards,
snakes, and alligators. With chalk she draws a Cuban flag

on the sidewalk and Patria y Vida on the cement post.
I shout VIDA as the life seeps out of my mother. She cannot
speak, or chew, or control her extremities.
I lift her leg stiffened by disease and exile and hold her jaw
steady to sip wondering if Tuesday will be the day.
I pray for a reprieve.
What is this life if not a wave that carries one's pain
and pride out to sea?
I will float like a mangrove seed. It can survive
up to a year and colonize other islands, even continents.

CREATION

after Judith Ortiz Cofer

The tide is so low I can walk along the ocean side
of the mile-long stacks of coquina slabs. Shifting

layers of time, in this miniature Grand Canyon, where
the waves carve out shallow pools within the gaps.

I cool off inside one, my back melding into wet sand.
An osprey soars, displaying its banded, arched wings,

its dangling catch. Grand contra azul, I forget to feel
sorry for its prey. Lazily, I turn, like the Great Blue

Heron wading through the water with its long legs near
the mossy rocks, verde. A spotless Snowy Egret joins

us. From my view between the rocks, I watch it sway
its head and flick its wings. It ambushes a shiny gray fish,

swallows it whole. El mar flows along my body. It drags
in more shell bits. Is this how it felt on the seventh day?

TWO POEMS: FOR WHEN YOU LOVE SOMEONE THE WAY I LOVE YOU

1.

Some types of weeds look nice
and can be good for pollinators
but they can also spread wildly
and drown an entire garden.

The more stubborn ones you pull
slowly and steadily easing the soil
to defend the grass and clover
the way you safeguard each of us.

After all the years, one would think
I knew everything about you
but yesterday you surprised me,
the way you yanked the roots

from those damaging memories
that had taken hold of us.

2.

On the shaded side of the house
where only weeds existed in mud
you shape a secret garden.
It's not really secret, one can see
it from the front porch, but it
holds the secrets of many loves.
A stream of turquoise river stones
spills onto the gravel path through

an entryway beneath the weeping
bottlebrush, its pendulous branches
lit by lights like fireflies at night
where I call you for a kiss
as if we stood under the mistletoe.
The passage continues beside
the firebush often visited
by hummingbirds and bees
until it reaches the white arch
framed in bougainvillea vines
above blue daze, ruby lantanas
and pink pentas like a sea of colors
under stars whispering blessings.

WATERWAY

My daughter's neighborhood is a rectangle, each
shaded sidewalk lined with carport houses, a canvas

for back home yarns or a refuge for the downpours
and the castaways. The eager streets are framed by three

busy roads, but mainly by a limestone canal, that shifts colors
while passing homes, bridges, parks, until opening to the bay, like

a pilgrim winding through people's longings, taking the measure of God.

MIAMI MELODIES IN LATE JULY

after Donald Fagen

Rumbles in the distance open the gray theme.

Slow and thick, *walk between the raindrop* drops —
      overlapping pool water circles, clear templates,
      sanderlings scurrying ahead of rising waves in low tide.

Suddenly, leaning — reaching into windows — areca giants,
      spoon mallets hitting upside down teakettles,
      drums of melted ice pouring over hangovers.

Then, glass beads speckled across giant elephant ears.

A steam bath in tropical foliage,
      sleep in your arms.

LOVE IN THE TIME OF COVID

1.

Take the express lane on the I-95 interstate.
Pull out your sunglasses to shield
you from sharp sky brightness.
Take them off when you reach Old Cutler's
sprawling banyans.
Put on your mask and enter the hallway up
the stairs to your place.
Turn on the screen to the Senate Chamber floor
reminding you of *Better Call Saul.*
Raise the volume. Drown out the sirens, honks,
reverse beeps, and outside chatter.
Take two aspirins to release the jaw pain
and rest before heading out again.

2.

Drive to the abandoned Chapman Field turned park
and walk between Australian pines and mangroves.
Watch the red hermit crab scurry back to wetness,
its massive claws poking from its borrowed shell,
and the egret leaning into the reflecting waterway.
Slowly absorb the greens resembling islands,
caterpillar-like toxins released.

3.

Go back to the apartment.
With afternoon delight over the treetops,
shoulders morphing into butterfly wings,
spent breaths in undercover stillness,
and the fragrance of a faraway melody,
hold these notes.

BOXED LACE

after the painting by Nicole Hospital-Medina

The black lace in the corner seeps
into the gray, like cubist breasts.

The sky is pink because the world
is upside down or maybe it's dusk

scraping the sea, a blue that flows
through pink on a crimson pole

until it breaches the gray. You exist
on a bright yellow square, an island

floating on rose petals retreating
from charcoal toward the blue rim.

That's where the wind and waves reside,
where you reside half wind, half sea.

TWINED

Evie drops her head on my chest, spilled milk all over her shirt. How vulnerable at one, determined to crawl or stumble her way through her older sister's world. June, wearing her dinosaur pajamas, is also sick, so I trudge to the neighborhood park pushing the double stroller. There, June slithers out of the seat carrying her plastic binoculars to observe tadpoles on the bank of the canal, while her sister looks on. Back at home, Evie still watching, I untangle June's curls to braid them, like I used to with their mother and before that my own. I tame the strands, until they fall down her back like a silk rope, like a lifetime of plans taking shape with each unexpected turn.

> *young jasmine vines cross*
> *right then left over middle*
> *tight and smooth sweet bonds*

THE WEDDING ARCH

You and I spend hours shaping it with pink roses and peonies,
and vines spilling over the wooden planks. We leave the arbor

leaning on the wall. Later, standing on each side of our daughter,
arm in arm, we round the oak walking over the grass in between

the rows of white chairs. The rose bower blooms against the forest,
as the three of us head toward the portal. She carries us to this place

where the woods stir love with fantasy, to these pangs of youth's urges,
before the daughters, before college, before parent anger and expected

church vows, to where I can breathe in our dream and hold the rush;
we kiss her and her beloved, then move away together – stabbed by joy.

MOVING DAY

Today you will tear open
cardboard boxes → slowly unravel
yourself → along with wedding
gifts and hopes → hidden beneath
rejection letters and journals

A poet writes that dusk
is an untrustworthy time →
what can we trust if not dusk
and the moon and the sun and
the surf with their timeliness →

I trust → the oaks and pines
rising outside your third floor
window → the thrill of morning's
empty boxes, unsealed utensils,
crisp shower curtains →

I trust you and me to be → just be
like the sharp needles of the bonsai
on your porch → no tree is too small
to trim, prune, and graft to → grant
a windswept juniper a glorious shape

OF DREAMS I SLEEP

Our big bed hovers, a throne
in the middle of a great hall,
unattended and ignored,
until I need it,
for dreams of healing,
for reading a rainy day,
for making love with love.
Outside the white rockers
swing with loneliness
flux and squat in an inhabited place,
risking something.

He makes the bed each morning
smoothing its edges like a mantle.
When he doesn't
and the covers spill
over the tile, I long for its usual
quieting presence, like a visitor
on a dark mood morning.

Especially at the end of a long day,
I am so glad, Procrustes, son of
Poseidon, the stretcher, doesn't need
his hammer to wedge us into our crowned
berth. I sigh with relief as I slip
deep into golden eagle feathers.

*Line in italics from *Schizophrene* by Bhanu Kapil

PROTECTING THE INTERIOR

for Maureen, diagnosed 2017

The moat, battlements, cannons, thick clam walls
kept Spaniards safe inside Castillo de San Marcos.

Nothing could protect you or me when our walls
failed leaving the interior unguarded from mutating

cells expanding to where they became unwelcome,
resistant to our weapons, unresponsive to our prayers.

The bastion diamond shaped design of the Fortaleza
along with its porous façade of tiny colorful coquina

absorbed or deflected projectiles, instead of yielding.
But how to control their spread once they are inside?

They circumvent the defenses, hide, recruit, and trick.
Perhaps a glowing clusterwink with its flashes of green

light might frighten or distract them, or at least grant
more time to restore, transform, and strengthen the fort.

SHIRTS WITH BAGS (AUSTRIA, 15TH CENTURY)

The word brassiere from the French "child's undershirt" shifted into bra.
In Ancient Egypt women wore bra-like garments over one or both breasts.

For 20 years, I have used a bra to cover one breast. Is that a unibra?
Most people would rather see a breast than a breast scar. Maybe not.
As soon as I can, I unsnap that devious garment that pulls and squeezes,
but without it, I'd be lopsided and slumping. And no one wants that.

At least it's not a corset, which replaced the earlier wears.
Three hundred years of cruel and unusually constraining punishment.

> *Burn up the corsets! ... you will never need whalebones again.*
> *Make a bonfire of the cruel steels that have lorded it over your*
> *thorax and abdomens for so many years.*
>   (Elizabeth Stuart Phelps Ward, "What to Wear")

The metal shortages in WWI boosted its end. War can have its benefits.
Thank you, Mary Phelps Jacob for a pair of silk handkerchiefs & ribbons.
At home alone, I hang free to roam from room to room beneath my cottons.

> *Wall paintings in Crete's Minoan civilization of 3,000 years*
> *ago show women performing athletics in bra-like garments*
> *that supported but also emphasized and enhanced their breasts.*
>   (Hawkins, "The Evolution of the Bra")

Breast sagging cannot be prevented with any garb. Blame smoking,
pregnancies, weight gain or loss, & of course, gravity! All sags in time.
Still, we excavate styles, fits and sizes for evidence of perky perfection.

Indian women used half-sleeved tight bodices since the 1st century: *kanchuka*.
The *dudou* in the Ming Dynasty was worn to flatten the breasts with grace.

In Somalia, wearing one is un-Islamic and has lead to whippings or arrests.

Back in the U.S.A. …

Flapper rayon bandeaus in the 20's; sweater girls in bullet bras in the 50's. Padding and underwire in the 60's; comfort, natural and sporty in the 70's.

By 2012, it's show the straps, add color; 2016, #freethenipple, avoid the device.

Me, I insert the silicon breast, snap the hooks, & head out for a beach swim.

Balance is restored.

THE CROSS THAT CARRIES US

Two years of nursing our youngest
was supposed to be the antidote.

Instead, the man I love is suddenly
married to a one-breasted woman.

Draining tubes and fainting needles,
carved out wounds and tossed pills,

metallic nausea and lopsided chest,
even thinning strands, all fade into fog,

but not the endless ledges and
premonitions, planks etched in

leafy dragons and feather stars
we haul until we reach the shore,

our beams refracted sea glass.

RINCÓN DE LA VIEJA NATIONAL PARK: SUMMER AFTER CANCER

on the way up the slope
of the Old Woman's Nook

        ceiba tree buttress roots
        a breathing backdrop

a digital clasp

climbing through thicket
mist cooling our sweat

        a view to a cliff
        we would have kissed

a water rush

closer to the summit
cracks and fissures

        steam and gas vents
        belching out clouds

a slow warning

PRIMER FOR DIAGRAMMING BREAST CANCER

Before breakfast, she confirms her biopsy is positive. Twenty-two years have passed since my own diagnosis, but the angst rises from the gut like a geyser. I want to assuage her fears, but I realize hers are scrambled and raw.

We review the functions:
A breast (sentence) is the largest independent unit of femaleness (grammar).
Its meaning is dependent on its structure: dense or not.
It helps to break down its components: ducts, lobules, and connective tissue.

<u>Woman | feels</u>
<u>Breast | flies</u>
<u>Breast | feeds | baby</u>
                   <u>milk</u>
Breast | makes | /
               \ them
             \h
            \a
            \p
            \p
            \y

<u>Breast | is \ aching</u>

My aching spreads, like the growing wildfires at Yosemite's Mariposa Grove, for her and the threatened 2,000-year-old sequoias towering 20 stories, irreplaceable. She wants it to stop quickly, to have it removed, and be done, so she can return to her previous life. I do not share that there is no going back. The diagnosis, like the blazes, will tattoo a firebrand.

REFRACTED

At 16, life was a black-and-white
film washed in shadows.
Vested uniform and stale homework,
parents at war, war abroad,
hearings and resignations.
I planned to make my way alone,
but without waves is there an ocean?
without moon, a night?
You came, pockets stuffed with colors.
Slowly you released them
and I held each one up to the light.

THERE IS NO TURNING

                                                Time
                                                        Time
                                                                     Time
                                                                                  Time
Time Time Time Time Time Time Time Time Time Time Time
                                                                                  Time
                                                                        Time
                                                            Time
                                                Time

no single measure for one place

I am the child I abandoned

yesterday ejects matter
I can't breathe   tomorrow
now, just is

mass	in my headstand on the sand my thoughts spill out slowly
motion	walk around me and you can catch them gradually
memory	upside down I won't forget your face

BLOODROUTE

for days we swerve into forest
we rise and fall with the granite slopes
skirting tree top cliffs,
the spine of the blue mountains
seizes our breath

curves, curves, and switchbacks

from the Smokies to the Shenandoah
we ride this asphalt artery
of the longest linear park unspoiled,
safeguarded, every mile a green meditation

from the topless jeep, we inhale the Appalachians
on both sides of this narrow ridge

curves, more curves, and switchbacks

at the highest point, rows and rows
of airy peak chains ripple the horizon,
skipping stones to heaven

at the lowest, by the banks of the James River,
intoxicating strokes of yellow pink white wildflowers
sway and hum beneath our feet

curves, more curves, and more switchbacks

in this half century-in-the making
bloodroute that tops crests,

reaches into valleys, crosses woods,
and now flows through us,
it took five days to lose and find ourselves

more curves, more curves, and more switchbacks

DRIVING BACK

We take a narrow gravel road along the river, so
close, you can open the door and step onto its bank.

Windows open, we slow down to listen and follow
its movement. No two rivers are alike, like you and me.

Two people long in love, no words are needed, we
quietly track the current, as if it were guiding us.

At an unexpected hanging footbridge, we pull over.
The path of planks and hanging chain links is swaying.

You walk ahead, to the other side, watching the water;
I move towards you, observing you, a man like a river.

Instinctively water flows, moving boulders or dead trunks,
pushing through tree walls, like veins, to reach its sea.

The footbridge ends on a forest island where the river forks.
Each side carrying all the things we still don't understand.

From there, across decades, you smile at me, and I recognize
the one I married unencumbered, at ease in this flow beneath

you. We meet in the middle. Here it is just us, our senses
rushed by blues and greens. We cross the river.

UNDER A STILL SKY

It is a light December day, so quiet, I can hear
myself breathe as the scissors thin in slow motion.

Clumps of gray drift across the floorboards
to the grass, like dreams you want to forget.

Nothing matters but each strand. The sun feels
gentler here in the shaded deck. In the front porch,

it takes aim, as we sway in the hammock. The heat
making us sleepy, I lean into you, a reflecting light.

Two yellow bellied flycatchers flitter over the red
bottlebrush blossoms. They are hovering, like us.

TODAY I HAVE COMPANY

we walk without words
      under a harvest moon
      towards sea
the rooster crows
the carpenter hammers
we swallow damp air
      and pink foam clouds
shore egrets wade
fishermen cast far
waves rise high
      beneath the saffron star
      ascending

we head back
      our shoulders
      baking
looking for shade
      to cool our
      skin
and the angst
      of shortening days
      yet to come
a wild rabbit
      scurries to hide
      in the scrub

GOING ON FIVE DECADES

for Carlos

You came to me afloat
laughter and song
risa y sones
your skin on mine startling my pores
lluvia like a sudden shower.
Now I have learned to read the rain
and your sighs suspiros,
heavy downpours or tender drizzles,
always sustaining gota a gota,
still gripping,
you reach for my hand,
anywhere,
dos manos
everywhere,
like two elements,
without the other,
there is no sea.
no hay mar
no hay más

TAKING TURNS

No one will save him who's never loved.
— Li-Young Lee

Hold my hand,
you say without words.
I reach for your joy,
and tremble.

You are a mirror in my pocket.
What if it breaks into shards?
Will it reflect in broken pieces?

Turn towards me,
you say with your body.
I try to memorize the steps.

You use words to pull me closer
and a hand on my waist to lead.

What if I'm called to steer alone?

Listen to the stories,
you say sorting photographs,
old lovers leaning on a skiff.
I do.
But they only exist in memories.

We are the story now,
you say, like the bamboo shoots
battered by surge and freeze,
still sprouting green.

We use few words in the light
and even less in the dark.
Your exhale is my inhale.

Two cardinals fly into the trees.
And my chest opens up slowly,
reminds me to take in the colors.

There is still time for more stories
until the sun sets.

EPILOGUE

BAND OF POETS

for Tres abuelas y una mamá (2016-2023)

Maureen went giddy calling ourselves a band
instead of just poets. Never did hit the road,

but in the Age of Covid, we had virtual gigs, all
hits. (I write in couplets because she loved twins.)

Imagine us a band. Maureen the rock keyboardist,
Holly the lead vocalist (what a voice this actress hides),

Nicole the grunge guitarist, and I the percussionist
(congas or bongos or maracas?) I said imagine.

We played words for two hours a week, for seven years.
Until we didn't.
                        silence

(Maureen really liked white space, parentheticals, and the sea.)

Grief settles on the waves, gently some days. I manage a breath
and take in sunlit clouds, on an absurdly blue sky, sweet world

of memory. Other days it explodes without warning, plunging
and collapsing, leaving no room for anything but bracing below.

Then sounds abandon rhythm, light shuns color, and echoes lose
their words. Words become untrustworthy, without angels.

Hay dolores en la vida, tan fuertes…   *!Yo no sé!**

(Maureen's last poems were written in Spanish. I don't know why.)

*from Cesar Vallejo's "Los Heraldos Negros"

ABOUT THE AUTHOR

CAROLINA HOSPITAL is a poet, prose writer, and editor. Her works include the poetry collections *Key West Nights and Other Aftershocks* (Anhinga Press) and *The Child of Exile: A Poetry Memoir* (Arte Público Press), as well as *Myth America* and *How to Get into Trouble* (Anhinga Press), both collaborative collections with Maureen Seaton, Holly Iglesias, and Nicole Hospital-Medina; plus, the novel *A Little Love*, under the pen name C. C. Medina (Warner Books). She also collaborated with South Florida writers on the *New York Times* bestselling novel *Naked Came the Manatee*. She edited *Los Atrevidos: Cuban American Writers* (Ediciones Ellas/Linden Lane Press), a groundbreaking anthology of Cuban Americans writing in English, as well as *A Century of Cuban Writers in Florida* (Pineapple Press). She wrote the lyrics to the song cycle *Greetings from Florida: Postcards from Paradise* by composer and UF Assistant Professor Scott Lee released as a CD. Her most recent poetry collection *Bamboo Ghost Notes* was published as a numbered limited edition by Contagioso Press.

www.ingramcontent.com/pod-product-compliance
Lightning Source LLC
Chambersburg PA
CBHW061802070526
44586CB00023B/2678